The Getter Group Guide

Everything You Need to Know About Buying Real Estate in Israel

Contents

About This Guide	1
Keys to a Successful Real Estate Purchase	2
Finding the Right Place	4
Building a Budget	8
Sealing the Deal	11
The Nuts and Bolts of Buying a Home	14
A Blueprint for Design	16
Making Those Payments	19
The Home Stretch of Your Apartment Purchase	22
Managing the Mortgage	24
Inspecting the Property	28
The Final Stages	30
The Key to the Keys	32
Delays and Compensation	35
Registration Complications	37

The Surprising Psychological Factors
Affecting Our Purchases   40
    The Fear Factor   42
    Unrealistic Hope   47
    False Expertise   52
    Seeking a Mirror?   55

The Hard Work of Good Decisions   58
    Getting Objective   60
    Maintaining Perspective   62

Our Services   63
    The Brokerage Service   64
    The Advocacy Service   65
    Ready to Make Buying in Israel a Whole Lot Easier?   66

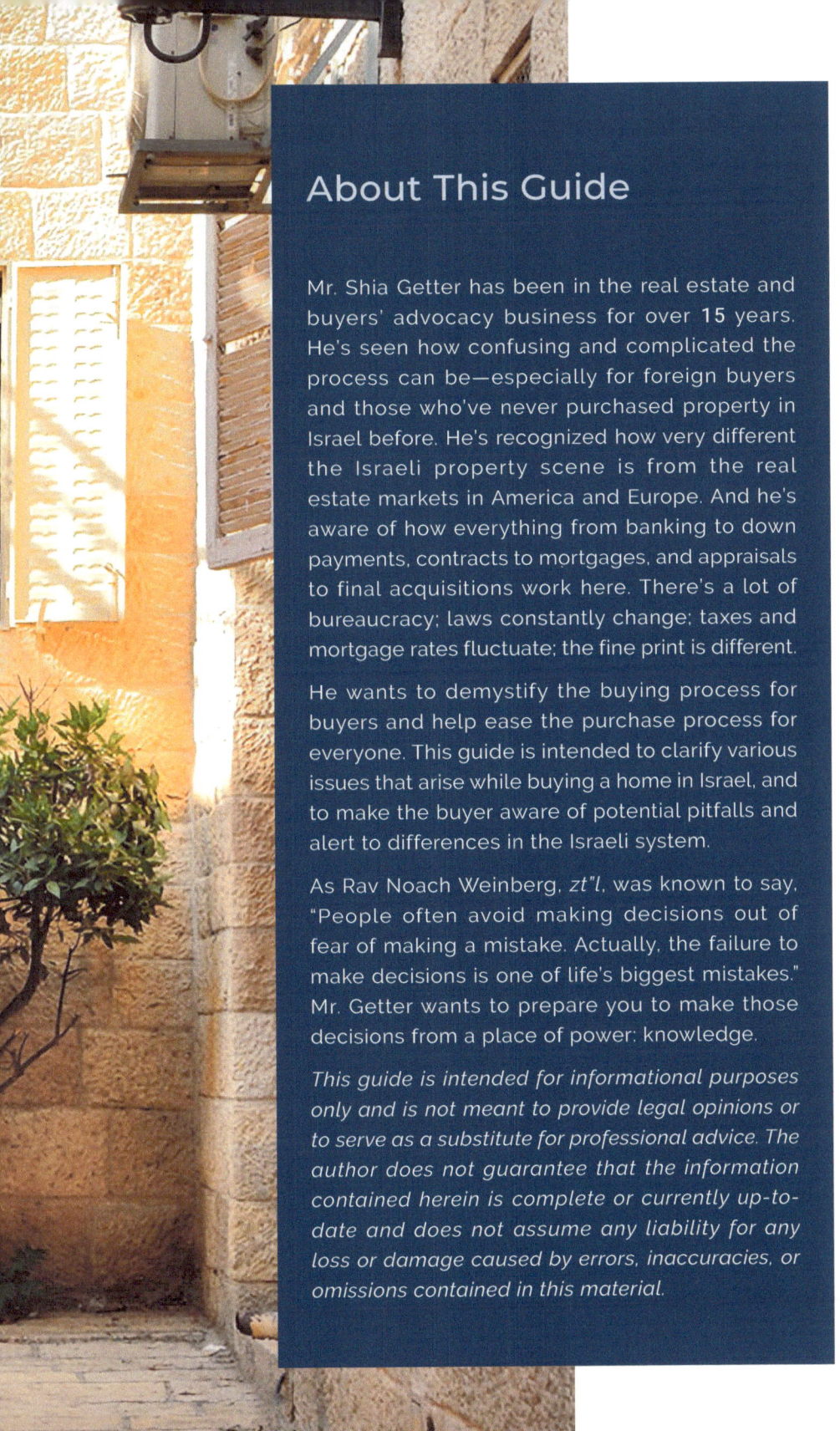

About This Guide

Mr. Shia Getter has been in the real estate and buyers' advocacy business for over 15 years. He's seen how confusing and complicated the process can be—especially for foreign buyers and those who've never purchased property in Israel before. He's recognized how very different the Israeli property scene is from the real estate markets in America and Europe. And he's aware of how everything from banking to down payments, contracts to mortgages, and appraisals to final acquisitions work here. There's a lot of bureaucracy; laws constantly change; taxes and mortgage rates fluctuate; the fine print is different.

He wants to demystify the buying process for buyers and help ease the purchase process for everyone. This guide is intended to clarify various issues that arise while buying a home in Israel, and to make the buyer aware of potential pitfalls and alert to differences in the Israeli system.

As Rav Noach Weinberg, *zt"l*, was known to say, "People often avoid making decisions out of fear of making a mistake. Actually, the failure to make decisions is one of life's biggest mistakes." Mr. Getter wants to prepare you to make those decisions from a place of power: knowledge.

This guide is intended for informational purposes only and is not meant to provide legal opinions or to serve as a substitute for professional advice. The author does not guarantee that the information contained herein is complete or currently up-to-date and does not assume any liability for any loss or damage caused by errors, inaccuracies, or omissions contained in this material.

Keys to a Successful Real Estate Purchase

1. Finding the Right Place
2. Building a Budget
3. Sealing the Deal

Finding the Right Place

"Location, location, location" is probably the most well-known—and clichéd—rule in the real-estate industry. Is this true—and what does this phrase mean anyway?

A home's location is one of the biggest determining factors in its desirability—and in whether a property will increase or decrease in value. What's often overlooked, though, is whether that "location, location, location" is in fact good for you. Even if a place is perfect on paper, do you actually want to live there?

When searching for a neighborhood, the single most important element is whether it meets the needs of your lifestyle. Sounds simple enough, right? But there are many aspects to examine:

- Is there a shul (or shuls) you feel comfortable davening in?
- Are the schools in line with your *chinuch* goals?
- Are the area residents people you would want to build relationships and socialize with?
- Are there easily accessible amenities, like grocery stores, medical facilities, and so on?
- What's the atmosphere like?

◉ Do you enjoy a suburban setting, maybe even with a view, or do you prefer the round-the-clock action of a fast-paced city environment?

  Does this neighborhood truly meet the needs of your lifestyle?

Though these questions may sound obvious, your answers to them form the foundation for your basic contentment, security, and wellbeing in any location. Visiting different neighborhoods and speaking to people who live there, davening in the shuls, and even just stopping by the local parks and shops can familiarize you with a neighborhood's atmosphere. Speaking to both long-term residents, as well as to people who moved in more recently, can help you get a feel for what the neighborhood was—and what it's becoming.

Additional features to look for are:

◉ the accessibility and convenience of public transportation and/or parking
◉ the overall aesthetics, upkeep, and cleanliness of the neighborhood
◉ how noisy (or quiet) it seems to be
◉ and whatever other factors are important to *you*.

  Make a list of your priorities for a neighborhood and number them in terms of importance.

After you get a feel for a place, it's easier to figure out what your highest priorities are.

What makes a place feel like home? What factors are non-negotiable? What delineates the lines you will not cross? As the saying goes, you can't have everything *you want – but you can have the things that really matter to you.*

Though it may sound overwhelming to speak to so many people and visit so many places, this *hishtadlus* is essential *before* you start looking at (and potentially falling in love with) apartments.

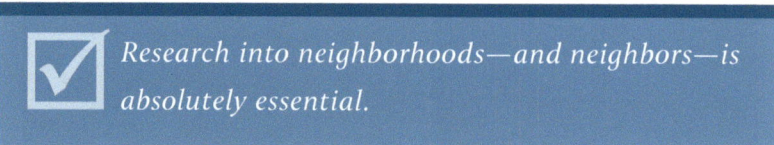

Research into neighborhoods—and neighbors—is absolutely essential.

There's an old saying, supposedly a Jewish proverb. "Ask about your neighbors, then buy the house." In Eretz Yisrael, neighbors play a very big role in a family's life, as the population density is high, and people are living in close quarters. This holds true even in many places where people are purchasing villas or single-family homes, which are often situated much closer together than they would be in America or Europe. So do your homework!

KEYS TO A SUCCESSFUL REAL ESTATE PURCHASE 7

And if you're looking to invest ...

If you're planning to purchase property solely as an investment, "location, location, location" also holds true. It's just that what makes that location ideal is a bit different:

- Does the neighborhood have a high—and growing—demand for rental properties?
- Is there lots of building and development taking place in that area?
- Will the market soon be flooded with other rentals?
- Is there a lockdown on new construction, meaning that every piece of existing property is absolutely precious?

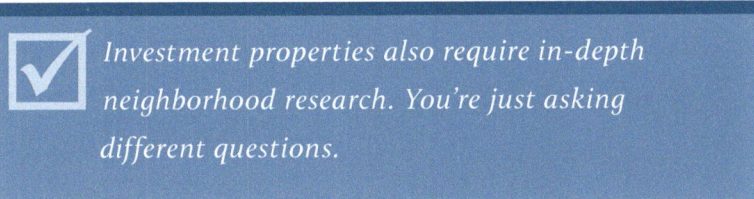

Investment properties also require in-depth neighborhood research. You're just asking different questions.

Regardless of whether you're looking for a forever home or a forever investment, enlisting professional assistance from a knowledgeable real estate group or a brokerage firm, like The Getter Group, is the way to go. Experts can give you an inside scoop—and an outside perspective—on what's really happening in any given real estate market, especially in a place like Eretz Yisrael, where being "in the know" means being on the road to success.

Building a Budget

Now that you've figured out where you want to buy, you need to figure out how to make that possible—and that all boils down to your budget. For that, you'll need both dollars and lots of sense; after all, budgeting is not just about the apartment's ticket price, it's also about calculating for the other expenses involved, from realtors' and lawyers' fees to upgrades, renovations, mortgage rates, inflation, and more. Pre-sold apartments, purchased prior to construction, can sometimes be costlier than anticipated, due to building-material price increases, delays, and other factors. So read on to learn just what smart budgeting is all about…

To avoid unexpected budgetary developments, plan to spend 17–19 percent more than the apartment's ticket price.
Go ahead, say "ouch" now, and then breathe a sigh of relief, recognizing that working this into your budget will help you in the end. With a solid number in mind, you can start searching for an apartment you can actually afford, both now and later, even if "surprises" pop up.

> **?** *How much can I truly afford? Include a 17–19 percent cushion in that number.*

Keep in mind that having a realistic, firm budget can make you into a stronger, savvier negotiator when presenting an offer on an apartment.

Realtors and sellers will quickly realize that you can't be pressured to raise your numbers.

Having a solid budget only makes you into a stronger negotiator.

Expect the unexpected.

A common pitfall that buyers often run into in Eretz Yisrael involves the problem of mortgages and bank appraisals. Buyers apply for a mortgage based on the seller's asking price, but when the bank appraises the apartment, the buyer may learn that according to "official" calculations, the bank considers the apartment to be worth significantly less than the market does. This leaves the buyer in a lurch—seeking a mortgage that's actually much higher than the appraiser determines they need. Hopefully, if the buyer budgeted higher for "hidden" expenses, this won't be a major issue if it arises.

Bank appraisals don't always match market prices. You may find yourself looking for a mortgage that's higher than the bank thinks you need.

Mortgage brokers are also of tremendous assistance in negotiating the best and most competitive rates.
Don't underestimate how much they can help you—and how much money they can save you. In Israel, a mortgage broker isn't a luxury; it's a necessity.

Mortgage brokers aren't a luxury. They're a necessity.

For additional advice and assistance on how to build a rock-solid budget, contact The Getter Group. We've got years of experience helping people in all aspects of the home purchase process.

Sealing the Deal

Coming to contract is undeniably exciting. It's the point where you know This. Is. Really. Happening. But we mustn't let the thrill and anticipation get in the way of sense and reason...

Once a buyer reaches the point of contract, we must hire a lawyer.

A thorough, carefully worded agreement makes all the difference. The Getter Group has seen countless examples over the years of how unique points can be incorporated into a contract to protect the buyer and prevent unpleasant surprises. Building on such experiences, The Getter Group has created a distinct contract appendix, which inventories exactly what is included in the deal – from fixtures to appliances and more. Additionally, The Getter Group has drafted numerous unique clauses and other safeguards that can be added to a contract to protect the buyer as needed.

A unique appendix can be included in your contract to inventory just what's part of the deal. Make sure your lawyer is drafting clauses to safeguard you!

>  *The appendix is often more important than the contract itself!*

An often-overlooked aspect of contracts is making sure that all the technical details are indeed correct.

Are the physical address, property size, and so on, as listed in the document consistent with the information registered in the municipality? Unbelievably, an apartment's address might not even correspond to the address listed in municipal records! We've seen firsthand how recording this kind of information in a contract shields the buyer from objectionable occurrences down the line.

> *Details in the contract must be consistent with those in the municipality.*

The Getter Group has seen too many unfortunate examples of signings getting delayed while fee timetables remain unrevised. What that means is that a buyer may need to remit payments within a week or two of signing, even though he anticipated having two or three months to begin sending the fees.

> *All payment schedules should be updated according to the actual date of signing.*

Once the contract is signed, it's signed. We can't emphasize enough the importance of a tight, solidly reviewed contract.

Buying a home is among the biggest—and most exciting—purchases a person makes in his lifetime. Some people would add that it's also among the most stressful. Indeed, acquiring land in Eretz Yisrael is a huge mitzvah—and Chazal describe it as one of the three things that are obtained with suffering (niknim b'yissurim).

Engaging the assistance of a brokerage firm like The Getter Group can change the whole experience. With careful planning and thorough review—and some help from a knowledgeable, trustworthy buyers' brokerage advocacy service—the process can be a smooth and even pleasant one. Then you can start making that perfect location into a warm and happy home.

The Nuts and Bolts of Buying a Home

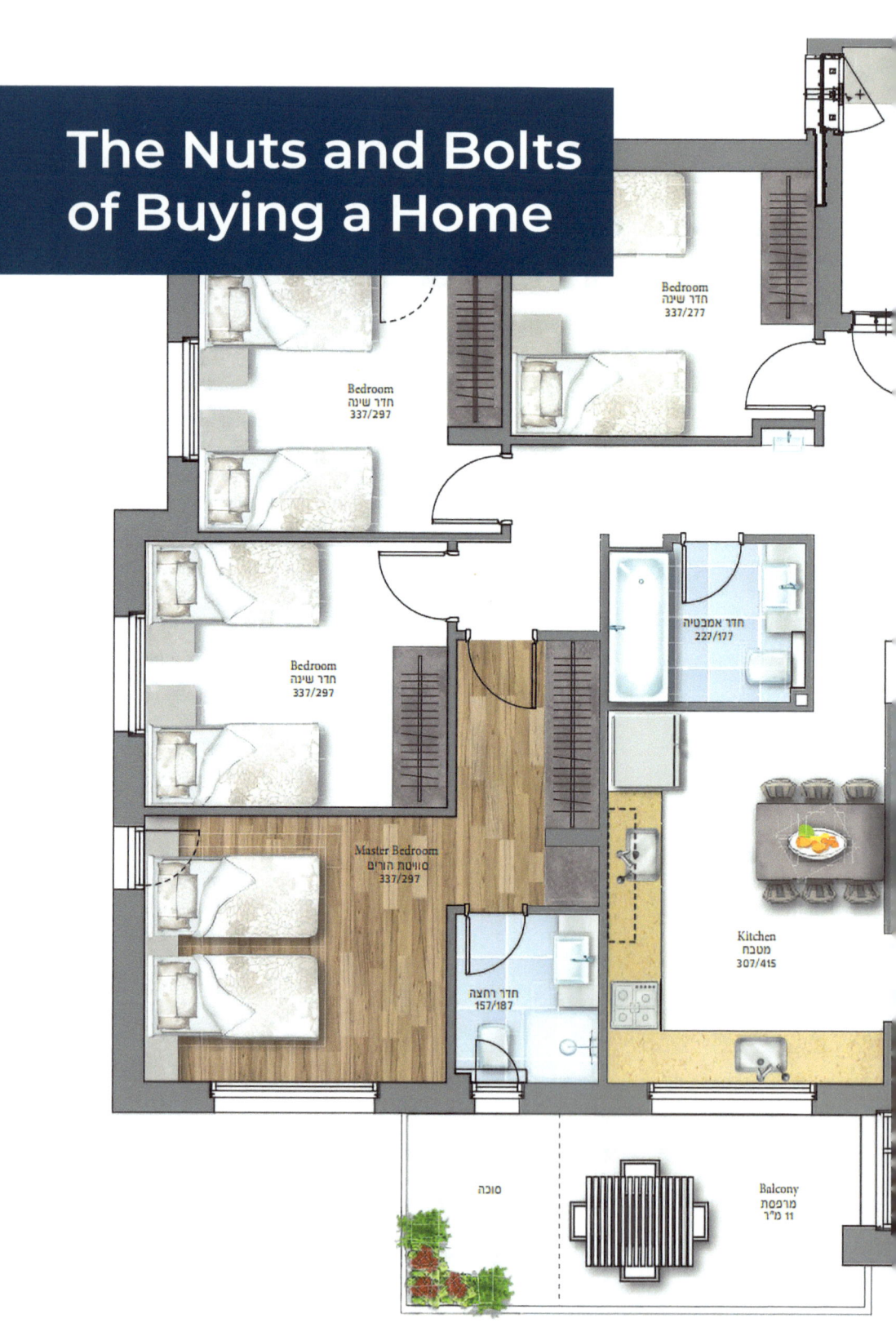

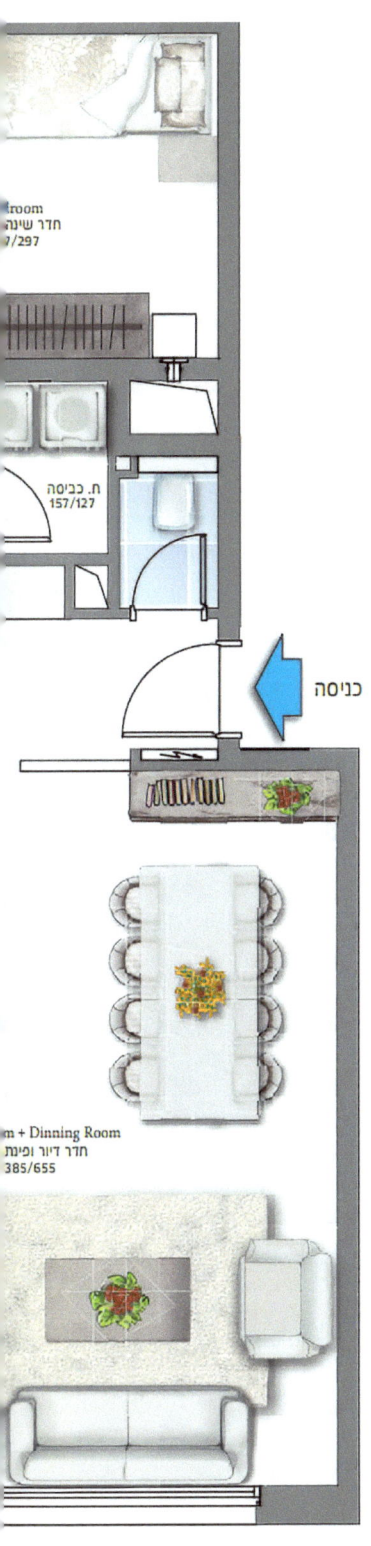

1. A Blueprint for Design

2. Making Those Payments

A Blueprint for Design

Designers often say that a home's interior should reflect the people who live there. And, of course, we also want to follow Chazal's dictate in Avos 1:4, "Make your home an assembling place for the wise and drink their words with zeal." But before we decide which artwork we're hanging where and what kind of draperies we want and, more importantly, where we're putting the sefarim shranks and how we're setting up the table, there are countless other elements to be arranged, down to a home's bones. This is especially true with new construction, as these apartments can be modified before a buyer even gets the keys.

Even if an apartment is purchased as an investment to be rented out, a knowledgeable designer can adapt the apartment to meet renters' needs, creating a space that will outlast many years of wear and tear.

 Find a designer who is truly qualified to help you, not just in terms of aesthetics but in terms of all the technical details.

A qualified professional can:

THE NUTS AND BOLTS OF BUYING A HOME   17

- Coordinate with the contractor, architect, electrician, and the many other tradesmen involved to review all the plans and updates.
- Examine the designs in conjunction with the physical structure of the apartment and the layout of the water and electricity supplies.
- Ensure all changes are up to code.
- Submit all drafts and plans according to the contractor's deadlines.
- Prioritize desired changes according to what is best done at what time, based on practicality, difficulty, and cost.
- Be present to make orders, arrange discounts, receive deliveries, verify warranties, and supervise installation.

> *Changes can often be made easily during renovations, but will be significantly more difficult and expensive if put off until later.*

If all this is making your head spin, engage the services of a trusted designer who works with professionals like The Getter Group. An added benefit is that The Getter Group follows up with the designer, making sure all plans are submitted according to schedule—and regulation. These aspects are just as important as—if not more important than—finding a designer with a great aesthetic.

> *People rarely regret renovations, changes, and updates they make. They often regret those that they didn't make. So, plan carefully!*

Remember, you want your home to tell the story of who you are—and not the story of the crazy disasters that happened in the process of designing it!

Making Those Payments

*If you calculated a budget and have funds for the down payment, what could be so complicated about transferring your money to Israel? For starts, you must find a reliable way to move that money from point A to point B. After all, you can't exactly stuff thousands of dollars into Uncle Shmeryl's suitcase! And you surely realize by now that **nothing can ever be simple.***

Transfer Service or Bank?

Many buyers prefer transfer services to banks. Here's why:

- To spare the trouble of opening an Israeli bank account at this stage
- To spend less, thanks to lower and fewer fees than banks
- To take advantage of competitive exchange rates
- To avoid "hidden" charges, for which banks are notorious
- To have someone managing payments to the seller or contractor, rather than doing it oneself
- To enjoy user-friendly, personal service (generally available in English, too)
- To reap the benefits of flexible hours, quick turnaround times, and more

>  *A transfer service may be the smartest way to send your money to Israel.*

What should you look out for when choosing a transfer service?

Find one that:

- Is licensed by Israel's Ministry of Finance
- Issues receipts
- Uses segregated accounts
- Has methods to secure the money
- Can hold your funds (or send them to an Israeli account)
- Will disburse the money to the seller (in the form of payment slips, or *shovarim*, in cases in which an apartment is purchased "on paper"), according to a designated schedule

> *Not all transfer services were created equal. Compare the benefits and services on offer before choosing.*

Beware the Taxman

An important factor, especially for U.S. citizens already residing in Israel, relates to potential tax ramifications that may arise when transferring money for payments. It's important to know the liabilities and laws.

THE NUTS AND BOLTS OF BUYING A HOME 21

- U.S. citizens who have over a certain monetary threshold in a foreign bank or investment account may be required to inform the IRS or face penalties.
- Foreign accounts, earned interest in foreign accounts, and the like may require disclosure on the buyer's U.S. tax returns.

> ❗ *Transferring large sums to Israel can lead to tax ramifications for U.S. citizens.*

Knowledgeable parties can ensure that a buyer is getting the best, safest deal on his transfer *and* can also scrutinize any legal issues involved.

Regardless of whether a buyer chooses to use a bank or a transfer service, if he employs a brokerage firm like The Getter Group, he will receive expert advice and guidance he can't get anywhere else, including which company to work with, when to exchange his money, and so much more.

The Home Stretch of Your Apartment Purchase

1. Managing the Mortgage
2. Inspecting the Property

Managing the Mortgage

Buying a home has been compared to finding your way through a maze, purchasing a used car, or even traversing a minefield. Whatever you want to compare it to, there are sure to be times you find yourself saying, "I didn't realize that" along the way… Let's walk through one of the most confusing areas to navigate: mortgages.

Most buyers require a mortgage to finance their apartment purchase. Even for those people who own other property elsewhere, the Israeli system can be perplexing and complicated. But don't worry: an informed buyer is the strongest buyer.

Most loans require a 50% deposit up front.
Make sure you can provide that down payment. The larger that deposit is, the lower your monthly mortgage fees will be. While first-time buyers who are residents of Israel can receive a mortgage for as much as **75%** of a home's price (and accordingly put down only a **25%** deposit), foreign buyers are eligible for mortgages covering only up to **50%** of the cost (and must furnish a **50%** deposit).

> **?** *Do you have enough money to make a 50 percent down payment on this property?*

Mortgages in Israel are available for a home's base price only.

A mortgage can't be increased to include fees, taxes, renovations, furnishings, and other associated costs, so you'll need to have separate funds set aside for those. (Of course, if a mortgage doesn't exceed the above-mentioned percentage, one can of course raise the amount to whatever limit the bank sets.) This *does* sound overwhelming and expensive, but if you make these calculations *before* you begin looking for an apartment, you should be able to find property that's not only comfortable to live in but will also be comfortable for your wallet.

> **?** *Have you set aside enough money to cover other expenses that won't be included in the mortgage?*

The Bank of Israel does not allow buyers to sign on a mortgage that requires payments amounting to more than 30% of their monthly income, in general.

Experts recommend building in an additional buffer to that amount, to account for fluctuating rates, income changes, and other variations in circumstance. These numbers should already give you a basic idea of what kind of mortgage you can afford.

> **?** *Is your recorded monthly income high enough to get the kind of mortgage you're seeking? (The mortgage can't be more than 30 percent of that income.)*

Individual buyers in Israel have little bargaining power when working directly with mortgage banks.

Occasionally, a person may not even be able to secure a mortgage on his own. And if he does, it will most likely not involve the most competitive rates or give him the best long-term value.

In Israel, a mortgage broker isn't a luxury.

Employing the services of a knowledgeable professional or a brokerage service like The Getter Group can save buyers an untold amount of hassle. In one recent incident, a client saved a whopping **$99,370** on a **12-year** mortgage thanks to The Getter Group's intervention.

Wondering how all this works? Professional mortgage brokers have the connections, leverage, and know-how to secure the most competitive rates, and they're familiar with the notorious fine print, which in Israel often lacks transparency. They can see the big picture, analyzing the market in the long run, often advising clients to take out long-term mortgages, understanding that apartment prices continue to rise, even as currency depreciates with inflation.

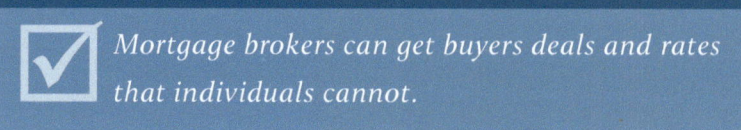

Mortgage brokers can get buyers deals and rates that individuals cannot.

Whether its research, inquiries, headache, or heartache – not to mention money – there's a lot at stake in the mortgage process, and a professional will look after and support you through it. Contact The Getter Group today to work with our mortgage broker.

Inspecting the Property

If only taking possession of your home could be as easy as making a **kinyan** *on the keys. And for those who buy an existing property, it usually is. After all, home inspections, engineer visits, and appraiser analysis would take place* **before** *signing the contract in such a purchase. But when an apartment is purchased "on paper," there's no apartment to check yet. All that must be done at the end.*

Inspection Time

1. When a newly built apartment is nearing the final stages of construction, the developer sends the buyer a letter informing him of such and letting him know that he should come and inspect his purchase.

2. The buyer usually has 30 days to make this inspection.

3. During such an inspection, the buyer should make note of whatever needs to be fixed prior to his move-in date.

Seeing Through Expert Eyes

At the inspection, the average nonprofessional buyer probably only notices things like poorly grouted tile or paint that needs touching up. *Unfortunately, some contractors take advantage of that relative unawareness.*

When a buyer brings in a professional to do the inspection, however, the check can be carried out in a much more thorough way. An engineer will notice if the construction isn't up to code, or if the tiling isn't properly level. Perhaps windows weren't sealed adequately—or at all, and the list goes on.

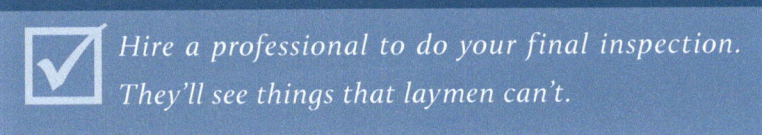

Hire a professional to do your final inspection. They'll see things that laymen can't.

Warning: if the original contract didn't have a clause allowing the buyer to bring in his own third-party inspector, the developer may prevent him from doing so. But when a buyer works with professionals like The Getter Group from the beginning of the process, he can be sure this right is solidly anchored in the contract. Not only that, The Getter Group finds and works with the engineers and appraisers to make sure the inspection is done properly—and in enough time for the contractor to make repairs.

Does the inspector always find something that requires repair or improvement? Yes, with a capital Y. But does the process have to feel like traversing a minefield? No. Not if you get help and go with a group like The Getter Group, who will advocate for you and walk with you every step of the way.

The Final Stages

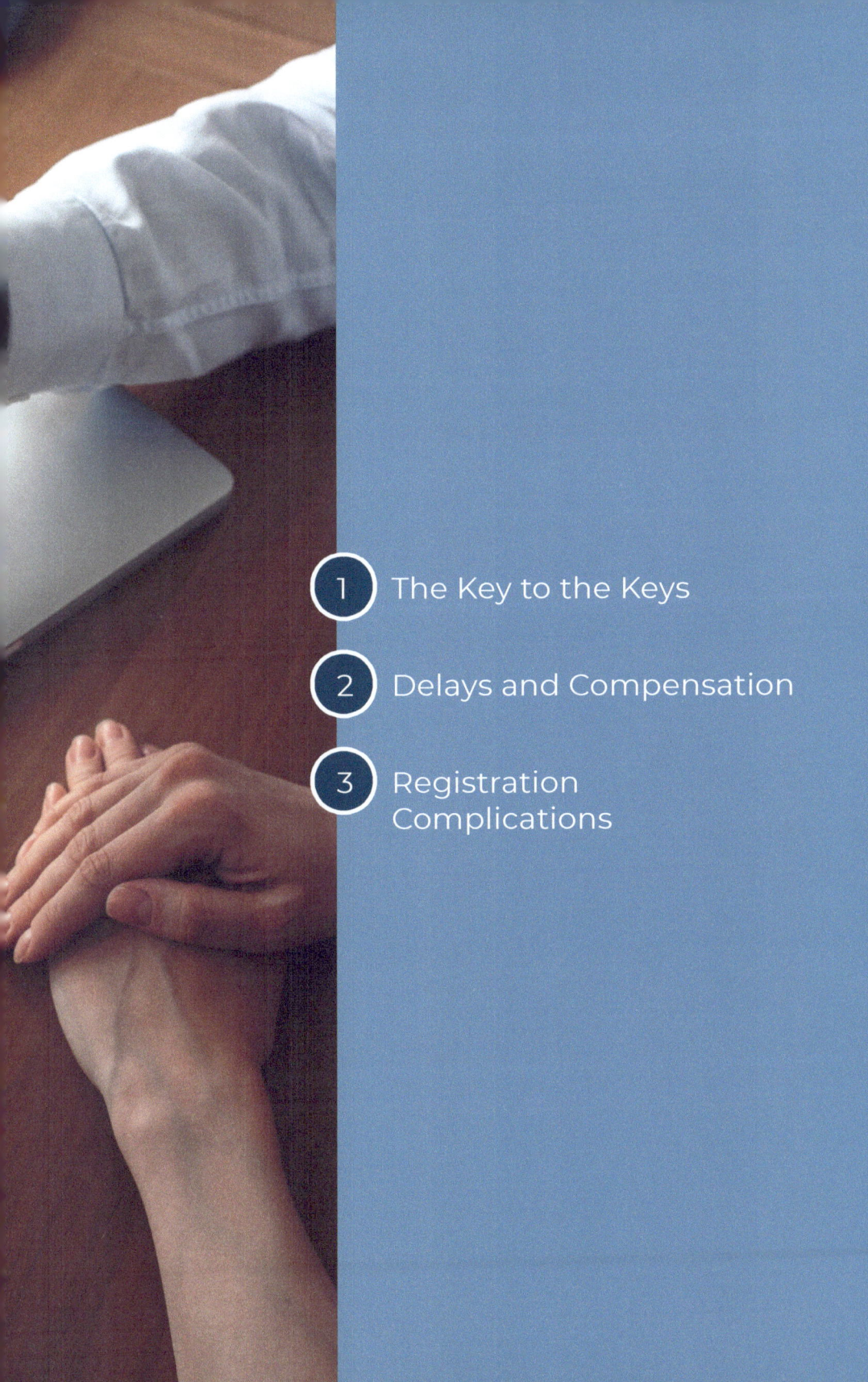

1. The Key to the Keys
2. Delays and Compensation
3. Registration Complications

The Key to the Keys

When a buyer purchases an apartment on paper and it nears the final stages of construction, the developer often encourages the buyer to come and take possession of his keys. The buyer is usually more than ready to get those keys in hand, likely having waited a good few years or more for his apartment and having suffered through numerous delays. Knowing that buyers are desperate to finally feel their keys jangling in hand, some developers unfortunately manipulate buyers into taking those keys as quickly as possible, even before an apartment is really ready for habitation.

Why Wait?

As soon as the keys are in the buyer's hand, the buyer must take full responsibility for coordinating the finishing touches on his apartment.

Surprise! That means the buyer must schedule all necessary repairs—and be present during them. If the developer sends various workers to make those updates, and the developer does so on his own schedule, the buyer can find himself doing a lot of waiting—and experiencing much frustration. **If the developer still has the keys in his possession, however, he is the one who must schedule, coordinate, and supervise the improvements.**

 Don't rush to take the keys. Make sure all repairs and updates have been finished first!

When the buyer takes ownership of the keys, the developer is released from the bank guarantees (and major pressure) related to that particular apartment.
Surprise again! That means the developer often lowers the priority level for finishing work on that apartment, preferring instead to complete *dirahs* for which he is still legally bound.

Unaware of this "nuance" (more like a game of hot potato), many individual buyers end up unwittingly celebrating the acquisition of their keys (*oops!*), when in fact they should be trying to *push off* receipt for as long as possible. (Who would have thought?) Of course, it's natural to want to take possession of one's property as soon as possible and to have what's rightfully his. As Rav Kahana says, "A person prefers to have one *kav* of his own produce, to nine *kavim* belonging to someone else" (*Bava Metzia* 38a). He just has to be smart about it.

In doubt as to whether you should take the keys or not? Ask the pros at The Getter Group.

Delays and Compensation

Ready for another "surprise"? New construction is usually delayed at some point. It's not always the developer's error; sometimes various permits or other bureaucratic procedures are at fault. (Blame bureaucracy!)

Waits & Indemnities: What You Should Know

- Developers have a grace period of **60** days to hand over an apartment after its estimated end date.
- Once those **60** days elapse, the buyer is entitled to receive *retroactive* compensation. (After all, this delay is costing him rent, and possibly other expenses as well.)
- The legally mandated compensation for such a delay is **1.5** times the price of rent for a similar-sized apartment in that locale.

Developers use numerous loopholes to avoid reimbursing buyers for the delays.
(Why is this not surprising?) Fortunately, the courts are usually on the buyers' side. If a buyer pursues legal action, the developer will generally come forward to work something out. Therefore, a buyer shouldn't be afraid of

hiring a lawyer to help him get that which he is legally entitled to. Don't worry; these cases rarely end up in court.

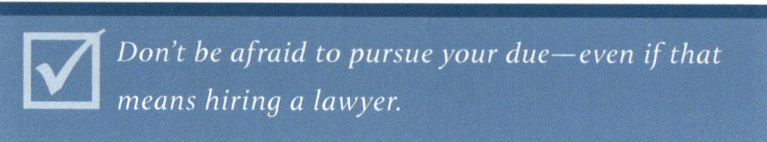
Don't be afraid to pursue your due—even if that means hiring a lawyer.

Other Reasons for Reimbursement

Delays aren't the only area in which a buyer is entitled to compensation. If, for example, a buyer installed a custom kitchen or bathroom in a newly constructed property, he should receive a credit for the builder-grade materials and supplies he would have automatically received from the developer. Unfortunately, it's usually the buyer's responsibility to pursue this refund and collect the money. (Add it to the list!)

If you're in doubt as to whether you're entitled to compensation or reimbursement, ask the experts at The Getter Group before proceeding.

Registration Complications

Registration sounds like it should be easy. Indeed, registering ownership of an existing property is as "simple" as going to the municipality and following all the regular bureaucratic procedures to get a home listed under one's name. But registration of newly constructed property can be quite complicated. (Not again!)

A developer can only legally register apartments in the owners' names once construction has been completed on an entire project.

Translation: All the apartments in a particular development must be built before they can be registered. This could sometimes take two years or more from the time the first apartments in a project are ready for occupancy. Therefore, a buyer must follow up and make sure his lawyer has finished all the necessary paperwork at the right time.

Municipal registration doesn't happen by itself—or automatically. Make sure to follow up!

While getting an apartment registered in one's name may sound like a strict formality, the legal ramifications can be great.

If a buyer wishes to resell the property or to refinance it later, an incomplete or non-existent registration can be a significant roadblock to that! Having an advocate in the picture—like The Getter Group—can mean the difference between these things being taken care of and being overlooked, between dotting all the i's and crossing all the t's and forgetting the details. Let someone else sweat the not-so-small stuff!

If an apartment isn't properly registered, it will be difficult to sell or refinance down the line.

The Surprising Psychological Factors Affecting Our Purchases

1. The Fear Factor
2. Unrealistic Hope
3. False Expertise
4. Seeking a Mirror?

The Fear Factor

*You want to buy a home because… Because… Well, you fill in the blank. Why **do** you want to buy a home? And if you're pulled toward a particular home and feel like you just.need.to.sign, ask yourself the same question: Why?*

Any marketer will say there's a lot of psychology that goes into every purchase. Home purchases, as big and life changing as they may be, are no different. What many home buyers find surprising, however, is just how big of an emotional driver fear can be.

What Are You Afraid Of?

There's a beautiful apartment for sale. The location is perfect. The neighbors are nice. The floorplan is just what you're looking for. It's a bit pricey, but… you feel like it's urgent to close the deal. Your subconscious starts playing games with you…

- *If you don't sign today, you'll lose out!*
- *Maybe someone else will snag it.*
- *The seller could change his mind!*
- *What if they raise the price even more?*

Or maybe you've seen a place that seems like a good fit, but you want to shop around and do more research. Then your agent warns you that prices are constantly rising in this location, that another buyer is seriously interested in the same apartment, that the seller is already discussing a higher asking price. Your agent's worrisome words ringing in your ears, concern worms its way into your heart, settling in your stomach.

- *What if this is your only chance?*
- *What if you miss out?*
- *What if…?*

Perhaps you've heard about a few people around town who've recently bought homes in Yerushalayim. After Maariv, you meet an old friend who mentions he's looking into property in Israel. Standing in line at the grocery store on Erev Shabbos, an acquaintance starts discussing his plans to get a retirement apartment… in Israel. It seems like everyone's buying in Israel these days! And there it is, that familiar old voice:

What about you, you, you?

> *Just why do I want to buy this place now? Is that a sound reason?*

Fear as a Psychological Driver

Fear is a powerful psychological factor in pushing purchases—even those as large and long-term as a home. **Loath as we are to admit it, emotion** *plays an even bigger role in our buying decisions than logic.* What that means is: **most purchasers make decisions based on feelings… and then attempt to justify them with logic after the fact.**

> **?** *What's motivating me? Am I attempting to justify my decisions ex post facto?*

Whether the fear emanates from within you, is implanted in you by a strongly sales-minded (and slightly manipulative) real estate agent, or emerges from heavy social pressure, it's there. FOMO (fear of missing out) is *real*. This fear can drive us to make rash, impulsive decisions without taking the time to do real research, get educated, or seek objective third-party opinions.

Fear can:

- drive a buyer to purchase a home they can't really afford.
- push a person to buy in a location they don't love.
- lead one to buy under conditions that aren't ideal.
- cause genuine buyer's remorse.

Being aware of this factor—and being aware of yourself and your emotional state—is crucial to keeping your head, heart, and housekeys beyond fear's grasp.

> **?** *Is FOMO a factor in your buying decisions?*

The Other Side of Fear: Analysis Paralysis

Although fear commonly pushes us to make hasty, even reckless choices, it can also do the opposite by paralyzing us. If you're not in the FOMO club—or even if you are—you may still recognize fear's equally unfriendly twin: anxiety.

- *Maybe, if you buy this home, something better will come up next week, next month, next year.*
- *Maybe, if you just wait a bit, you can get a better price.*
- *Maybe this place isn't as good as it seems and you're missing something huge and this whole purchase will be an absolute disaster?*
- *Maybe… Maybe… Maybe …*

When excessive caution becomes unjustified panic, you're left paralyzed. Instead of being ready to choose, sign, and move, such purchasers find themselves stuck, chronically hesitating… and *always* losing out. Just as much as FOMO is real, so is analysis paralysis. And it can keep you from ever acting and living out your dreams.

> *Is anxiety preventing you from making important choices? Is over-analyzing inhibiting you from moving forward?*

Somewhere in Between

Fear not, my friend. Somewhere between that risk-taking FOMO place and that immobilizing anxiety lies the sweet spot. When you really learn about your purchase options, including locations, pricing, mortgages, real value, and more, you can make choices from a position of power, knowing you're reaching a wise and educated decision.

Increasing your knowledge and mining for information can help you shop smarter when it comes to investing in a home. And you can enlist the help of the professionals at The Getter Group to do that research for you, presenting you with the best choices around. We'll give you the feedback and objective advice you need to make the most educated decision possible.

When you *do* find the right home, you'll be ready to sign with confidence, knowing you're making the right (and logical) choice. And what could be better than having real self-assurance in your decisions? (Other than moving into your dream home in Israel, of course!)

Don't let fear be a factor. Let us stand by your side.

Unrealistic Hope

Mr. Gould had found the perfect apartment. It was just what he was looking for in terms of location, size, view, neighborhood. He closed his eyes a moment. Yes, he thought, *I see us living **right here***.

There was just one tiny little… snag, if you will… And that was… the price. It was completely beyond the Gould family's means and range.

But… but…

Mr. Gould closed his eyes again. He could picture his wife kindling the **Shabbos licht** *right over there… And the children would sit on the balcony watching the street below. He would be able to get to work and his night* **kollel** *in no time… Everything was perfect.*

So, nu, nu. Money! It will work out. It's only money! Everything will be okay.

He nodded. This really was perfect. *"Hakol yiyeh beseder,"* he murmured.

Meanwhile, across town, Mr. Shapiro was sitting in a comfy leather chair at the beautiful mahogany desk of the sales agent in the well-appointed offices of Holy Properties & Development, Ltd. Mr. Shapiro looked around him, fingering the heavy black-and-gold pen on the *desk. These people had been so nice and helpful throughout the process. They seemed **100** percent trustworthy and competent. Surely, he didn't need to look into this further.*

True, he didn't understand all the fine print completely, but who does? And he had heard enough warnings to tread cautiously when buying property in Israel, but maybe these talebearers were just biased because they personally had had such bad experiences?

This firm had a good reputation, and Mr. Shapiro was pretty sure he'd heard great things about the other projects completed by their contractor. Besides, he was only signing a memorandum of understanding here… It wasn't like he was signing in blood! And everyone was always telling him he was a great judge of character…

*Mr. Shapiro looked into the smiling, encouraging face of the sales rep and nodded. He poised the pen that he'd been toying with and signed with a flourish. **"Hakol yiyeh beseder."** The words flowed from his mouth, smooth as the pen's black ink. After all, there really wasn't anything to worry about, was there?*

What's Unrealistic Over Here?

Unrealistic hope is a feeling we cling to when we get ourselves into situations we probably shouldn't be in in the first place.
When things start to get sticky or a bit uncomfortable, we may turn a blind eye to our discomfort and instead look to this insidious pretender called Unrealistic Hope. Mr. Unrealistic Hope wants us to just keep telling ourselves that everything will be okay… even when we didn't do our due diligence and we didn't do the necessary *hishtadlus* and we don't actually have any guarantee that anything will be okay.

> *Am I moving in a certain direction because I did research and know that it's a logical and sound choice? Or am I making decisions based off vacuous hopes and imagined outcomes?*

Unrealistic hope is a delusion we bring onto ourselves, an unstable feeling of joy we create based on an imagined future.
Whereas real hope is grounded in reality, unrealistic hope stems from distortions of reality. And unrealistic hope is one of the most common drivers of risky home purchasing decisions. It's what causes us to:

- look the other way
- neglect to do research
- ignore problems
- pretend we can afford things that are way beyond the budget

Legitimate Aspiration or Pipe Dream?

Someone sees a beautiful apartment or hears about the "perfect" new project going up. If the specs look good and it seems like a decent fit, what's unrealistic about wanting to buy in? Maybe nothing. Maybe everything.

Here's what you need to research and dig deep into *before* deciding what's sensible and wise versus what's unreasonable and illogical:

- the seller (or contractor)
- the neighborhood and general area
- the local pricing for various types of properties
- the building itself
- the materials, internal infrastructure, engineering, and general state of the apartment
- the engineers, architects, and other professionals involved
- the needs *you* have, including your budget
- the contract and other documents

And the list goes on...

> In-depth research and hard facts will help you ascertain whether a property is a sound investment — or if you're just dreaming.

The main differentiator between unrealistic hope and healthy hope is *education*.

If you're educated about all the relevant information, you're in a place to make a well-informed and realistic decision, and to truly hope that everything *will* indeed work out okay. Without vital information or when ignoring key factors, hoping everything will be okay is just… ignorant and unworkable. Ouch! (Let's not think about what happened to poor Mr. Gould and Mr. Shapiro. Suffice it to say their stories could drag on for years, cost them tens of thousands of dollars more than necessary, and even end up in *beis din*.)

Buying a home is one of the toughest and biggest decisions you'll ever make. Don't delude yourself by getting caught in the grips of unrealistic hope.

Do in-depth research. Get fully educated. Carefully examine the issue from all sides. Enlist The Getter Group to do it for you and walk with you through the entire process. And then you can know that, with siyatta diShamaya, everything really will be okay.

False Expertise

*Mr. Gordon knows **this is the year** he'll finally buy in Israel. He's really and truly ready. Having recently watched his two brothers-in-law purchase apartments in Yerushalayim, and now having seen his best friend go through the process, Mr. Gordon feels like he's practically been through it himself. He's even read tons on the topic… So, when a good opportunity arises, Mr. Gordon doesn't think twice or even seek another opinion. And why should he? He's virtually an expert on the topic…*

Maybe this scenario sounds exaggerated. But stories like this happen all the time—and not just to the foolhardy. **Our brains are hardwired to take shortcuts, especially when it comes to making tough decisions.** These neural shortcuts allow our unconscious mind to deal with a lot of incoming information—while leaving the conscious mind to make decisions. These shortcuts are really helpful. They're what make us duck when we see an object flying at our head and so on. But the same shortcuts can also lead us to make poor choices; they can cause us to put stock in *false expertise*, including our own.

- *Did you ever notice that your eye is naturally drawn to the person wearing the brightest colors?*
- *Or you pay attention to the loudest person in a room?*
- *Or you spot the tallest people in a crowd first?*

Even if they're not offering anything worthwhile or useful, we just pay them more attention. Why? Blame your brain and those shortcuts.

False expertise is misidentified competence.

- We (subconsciously) avoid doing the harder work of seeking out real experts.
- We look where it's easiest to find a "pro," perceiving expertise where there is none, or evaluating proficiency using irrelevant measures.
- We look to friends or acquaintances because they're convenient and accessible, rather than researching and contacting true pros.
- We even look to ourselves, convincing ourselves we have the experience, knowledge, familiarity, whatever—even when we don't.

> *What makes a person an expert? Are the people you're looking to for advice real experts? What are their qualifications?*

Even when *everyone* in a group recognizes who the true expert is on a particular topic, research shows that 40 percent of the time, the group still defers to the most extroverted person, even if he has no real experience in the matter. Other studies have shown that "airtime," i.e., the quantity of time spent talking, is a greater indicator of perceived influence than actual expertise. Kind of shocking, right?!

Guess who is the loudest, most frequently heard voice in your head? Uh-huh. It *is* easier to just trust our own instinct and believe in our own research, experience, and expertise, especially because we often overestimate our own knowledge.

We owe ourselves intellectual honesty.

Are we overclaiming?

Professing to know things we really don't?

People who believe they know more than they actually do are less inclined to pursue further education or seek advice from others. Something to bear in mind—and avoid! Need an expert opinion? You know where to go. The Getter Group's here for you.

Seeking a Mirror?

*The Klein family was super close to signing on a **dirah** in the new Prestige Project. "Maybe we should just get another opinion on it," Mrs. Klein said to her husband.*

Though the Prestige Project was most reputable and the company's lawyer top-notch, Mr. Klein agreed. He immediately called his old yeshivah buddy.

*He and Menachem not only went back years and years, they saw eye-to-eye on everything from current events to **hashkafah**, from food to investments. And he could trust Menachem with this personal information.*

As soon as Menachem heard about Prestige, he concurred with Mr. Klein. "A great idea! If I had the money, I'd do it myself."

Mr. Klein shouldn't have gone to Menachem. Instead, he should have approached someone who'd challenge his opinion and ask tough questions.

Mr. Klein had been "seeking a mirror," falling victim to "looking-glass merit." It's natural to seek validation.

When we find someone who agrees with us or is like us, it reinforces our own value. This unfortunately leads us to choose confidants and advisers based on similarity—not merit.

> **?** *Are you seeking advice from people who will challenge your opinions? Or are you just looking for validation?*

In such a scenario, we've already made our minds up. Now we just need someone—some just like us—to reassure us and confirm our choice. This is a kind of *confirmation bias*; we already think something is right or good for us, so now we just need to find evidence (or yes-men) to prove we're right.

Seeking the advice of like-minded people feels good, making us think we're correct and our decisions are justified. But this isn't necessarily so... Don't seek a mirror or jump through the looking glass. Seek someone to look out *for* you—someone like The Getter Group.

The Hard Work of Good Decisions

1. Getting Objective

2. Maintaining Perspective

3. Ready to Make Buying in Israel a Whole Lot Easier?

Getting Objective

Important decisions are usually the most stressful to make. They're multifactorial and involve much uncertainty and usually some time pressure, as well. With no single right answer and an overabundance of information at our fingertips (often from conflicting sources!), making those choices can become downright overwhelming.

Enlisting the help of an expert to present the relevant data and reliable information, and to sift through all the "noise," isn't a luxury. It's just smart.

Thomas C. Redman, president of Data Quality Solutions, wrote in the *Harvard Business Review*,[1] "Before you jump to a decision, you should ask yourself, '**Should someone else who has time to assemble a complete picture make this decision?**'" He says you should also be asking yourself, "**Do I really have a broad enough perspective to make and defend this decision?**" He advises asking yourself, "**What would happen if I moved in the *opposite* direction of my original choice?**" He adds that you should even gather data to defend that opposite viewpoint. Then he suggests reevaluating your decisions with *all* that data. Of course, we don't need Mr. Redman to tell us this. As the Gemara says, "Who is the wise person? The one who anticipates the consequences" (*Tamid* 32a).

---

1 March 10, 2017. "Root Out Bias from Your Decision-Making Process."

It's a big job. But it's the wise way to do things. Or, as Redman says, you can **"just get the right people involved"** and **"subject your thinking to someone who will really challenge it."**

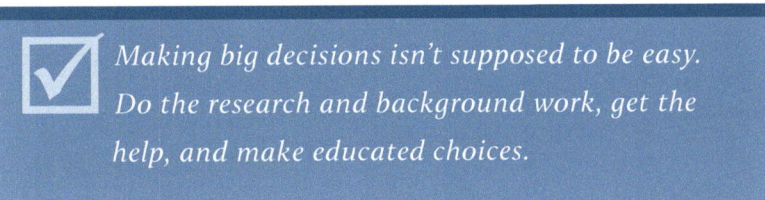

Making big decisions isn't supposed to be easy. Do the research and background work, get the help, and make educated choices.

The Getter Group will *not* make your decisions for you. But we'll ask the tough questions. And we'll present the full perspective. We'll piece together that complete picture, giving you the background and relevant data to make educated decisions.

You'll know why you're making your choice, you'll be doing it from a place of strength, and you'll be going through a real process to arrive at your answer. Get the right people involved. Call The Getter Group.

Maintaining Perspective

When there are so many details to be attended to and so many points to keep track of, it's easy to lose sight of the big picture: **you're buying an apartment in Eretz Hakodesh!** As the Gemara says, "The world is like an inn, the World to Come like home" (*Moed Katan* 9b). Keeping that end goal of a home in Eretz Yisrael in mind—and getting the professional assistance you need—can ease the process significantly. The Getter Group is here to help you see it through, from finding a place, to signing a contract, from inspecting your property to receiving the keys—and beyond. Keeping the end goal in mind can give you strength to jump through all the hoops and go through the process.

Purchasing a home is a big *brachah*, one that you will, *be'ezras Hashem*, be able to enjoy very soon. One day, all the hard work, decision making, bureaucracy, and negotiating will be distant memories (and hopefully good ones, thanks to The Getter Group).

It is with a heartfelt *tefillah* that we daven that the new memories we create in our homes should be of growth and happiness, from the moment we put up our mezuzos *ad me'ah ve'esrim*.

Our Services

For People Who Want to Do It Right

Simplifying the Purchase Process in Israel

The Brokerage Service

Locating, researching, advising

We:

- Listen to you, creating a unique picture of your wants and needs.
- See a thorough understanding of your preferences as prerequisites to finding the perfect place.
- Are exclusive to you, searching independently and impartially for apartments, without ties to specific listings, developers, projects, or agencies.
- View in-depth research as essential.
- Provide a perspective on all the nuances, coming from 15+ years' experience.
- Care about your budget and bottom line, never pushing or pressuring.
- Send you regular updates, including photos and/or video tours.
- Create a competitive analysis, with cost comparison tables and price breakdowns so you'll know the true value of a place.
- Help you make informed decisions based on real facts — not scare tactics.
- Believe in true wins: when both sides are happy with the outcome.
- Stand with you even after the contract is signed, until you've got the keys in hand.

The Advocacy Service

Guiding, representing, empowering

We:

→ Arrange a vetted mortgage broker; get your homeowner's loan on the best possible terms.
→ Review your contract for weaknesses and other issues.
→ Include our unique appendix & clauses in the contract to protect you.
→ Assist with service providers (banks, appraisers, and others), ensuring you get the best possible service.
→ Communicate with all parties on your behalf; you only need to speak with us.
→ Connect you with a trusted lawyer and manage those communications on your behalf.
→ Process payments by opening bank accounts, meeting payment schedules, remitting fees, and more.
→ Do the paper shuffle for you by handling the bureaucracy.
→ Coordinate & collaborate with all the other pros you need (architects, contractors, designers, engineers, and more).
→ Follow up as long as necessary, safeguarding your rights & entitlements.

Ready to Make Buying in Israel a Whole Lot Easier?

THE GETTER GROUP LTD.

will help you buy property
in **Eretz Yisrael**
and ease you through the process
with
menuchas hanefesh and
yishuv hadaas.

Contact us today.

Israel: 077-234-6011 | U.S.: (718) 473-3950 | U.K.: (020) 8150-6082
mail@thegettergroup.com | +972 58-318-0000 | thegettergroup.com
21 Rechov Petach Tikva | Jerusalem | 94474

www.ingramcontent.com/pod-product-compliance
Lightning Source LLC
Chambersburg PA
CBHW040230220526

45473CB00001B/186